Your Epic Encore

It's Never Too Late!

Rewrite Your Story
& Create The Life
Of Your Dreams!

Cheryl Broughton

Your

Epic Encore

Your

Epic Encore

It's Never Too Late!
Rewrite Your Story &
Create The Life Of Your Dreams!

Cheryl Broughton

Copyright © 2021 by Cheryl Broughton

ISBN: 978-0-578-58191-0

Printed in the United States of America

CDB Global Media
25852 Mc Bean Parkway #734
Valencia, CA 91355

"The Meaning Of Life
   Is To Find Your Gift.
   The Purpose Of Life
   Is To Give It Away."

—William Shakespeare."

This Book Is Dedicated With Love To:

Bobby & Patsy Broughton
My parents who taught me that anything in life is possible and that it's never too late to dream big. Your unwavering support is what has helped me through the toughest times in my life. You are two of the most caring, loving and humble people I know. Thank you for always being there for me. I feel so blessed that you are healthy, happy and still a movin' and a groovin'! I love you both so much!

Summer Davies
My beautiful, mermaid friend who reminds me to live life with a child-like abandon. My friend who has been with me on my ups and my downs. My friend who invites me on wild aerial adventures suspended over lakes, under waterfalls, between mountain peaks as well as lake surfing, roller skating, being mermaids and much more! Thank you for never saying, "Do you think you're physically able to do this?" Instead, it's always "I have this idea… and how soon can you be ready?" Love you girl!

Nick Rodriguez
Words can not express my gratitude for your support.
You have been my biggest cheerleader since the day we met.
You have always been there for me - giving me words of encouragement and sharing your wisdom. You are my rock, you lift me up and you make me feel like anything is possible.
Love you endlessly.

Contents

Foreword

"Your Epic Encore is an encouraging exhortation by Cheryl Broughton, who I have known for 35 years. She has been an inspiration, coach, example, nutritionist, to this seasoned Senior Tri-Athlete who has completed in over 200 triathlons, including 15 Ironmans. Ms. Broughtons' coaching through Your Epic Encore will not only get you to the finish line but motivated to get to the starting line no matter your age or circumstance..... The pain of discipline is sweeter than the pain of regret."

- David Sitton

4x Ironman World Championship, 4x Ironman Canada,
3x Ironman Florida, 3x Great Floridian Ironman, Utah Ironman,
5x NYC Marathon, 4x Boston Marathon.

Acknowledgments

I want to thank my closest friends and family, who have known me for years and continue to support me: Danny, David, Heather, Jeremy, Candice, Jen, Hugo, Theresa, Taylor, Angie, Sue Ann, Regina, Vickie, D.L., Tino, Eva, Steve, Carol & Kelly. And thank you to all my wonderful aerial students, my boot camp troopers, and my FE TV show crew who have supported me along this book-writing journey!

My Book Launch Crew:
Your words of wisdom and belief in me has helped me sprout new wings - more than you'll ever know! Alexa Freeburg, Candice Morgan, Wendy Lynn, Kristi Gaunt, Janice Wheeler, Betsy Asmus, Jo Mauro, Lizza Jacobs, Paula Richer, Sina Suemoto, Kareen Borzone, and Sandra Tatum. Sensei Subira - thank you for your guidance and unwavering support! And a big thank you in advance to all of those who join my team after this book is published.

Keala Kanae
Thank you for being so innovative and forward-thinking. Thank you for being "that guy" who once worked at a coffee shop but had dreams bigger than life. Thank you for never giving up and never letting anything get in the way of you creating this amazing program that has transformed thousands of lives around the world.

Kareen Borzone
"Choose and Move!" …These words will be imprinted on my brain forever! Thank you for being that bold, powerful, strong, no BS woman and mentor that I was searching for. Thank you for giving so much of yourself so that others can create the life they've always wanted.

Jimmy Campbell
"Team Jimmaaaaaay!" - I have thoroughly enjoyed learning from you. You have a way with people and know how to pull out their best potential. You are such a great example for all of us to follow.

Todd Campbell
Thank you from the bottom of my heart. You have changed so many lives for the better, and I am eternally grateful for finding you.

My AC3 Crew
I love you all, I miss you all, and I will never forget the bonds that were created and the unlimited amount of adventures and breakthroughs we all shared together. I think about you often and look forward to a reunion!

Carol Faltis
My fun, adventurous friend who acted younger than me but was older than me! 'lol' Thank you for showing me how to enjoy life and to live in the moment. Thank you for being one of my very first mentors who taught me so many valuable lessons! I can still hear you saying, "Cheryl, just trust me, I've been there!"
Here's to C&C Party Factory!

Introduction

Who Is Cheryl Broughton & Why Should I Read This Book?

Hi, my name is Cheryl Broughton, and you might be wondering, "Who is this Cheryl girl? How can she possibly help me with my goals, wishes, and aspirations?"

This book is for people who want a do-over, a reinvention, a new lease on life, a different outlook on life, and much more! I guess you could call it - an Epic Encore!

If your life is already amazing - then great! What are you going to do to ensure it stays that way when and if a "bump in the road" tries to knock you off track?

I have been helping people with personal transformations since the late 90s and dealing with my own personal battles along the way.

I've had many successes and many failures. And at one point, I learned to stop calling them "failures." Instead, I discovered that these were a series of auto-corrections by life trying to get me back on course, back to doing what it is truly in alignment with my highest values.

For this book to make any kind of impact or impression on you, I thought I would start by sharing my personal story of how I overcame some of the most challenging and darkest points in my life and the lessons I've learned. Then we'll transition into the steps you can take to create your very own Epic Encore.

I hope that you will find something you can grab onto, something you can relate to that helps ignite your own fire from within. Many times in our lives, all it takes is one story, one example that helps create a shift in our thinking and our outlook on life.

It is my goal and my mission to inspire you and to help you think outside of the box, to get past negative beliefs, and to help you take more effective steps towards creating an exponential life.

So, here are just a few of the many life lessons that occurred along my journeys and how I first got started in reinvention and personal transformations.

When I was 16 years old, I read a book that had a profound effect on me. It had a chapter on visualization. It talked about how you can mold your future by visualizing what you want to happen before it happens. You could open up doors of opportunity, get past negative people and situations, and could also use it for healing your body and strengthening your immunity and much more.

What was crazy was that it worked! I used it often when taking tests in high school or with pageants that I entered or situations at work. I also learned the hard way, that it only works when you apply it consistently, and that it's not the "end all, be all" for creating your future.

I loved growing up in the small town of Millington, Tennessee. However, by the age of 19, I was ready to get out and moved to Atlanta, Georgia. Then two years later to Myrtle Beach, South Carolina. That is where I started my self-improvement journey with a group of friends (around the early 90s). Being that our funds were tight, we would buy one authors' program, and we would share the cassette tapes with each other. Our homework was to take home one cassette, listen, take notes, and then recap what we had learned the following week.

We called our group LWP; live with passion. We would listen to Tony Robbins, Shakti Gawain, Dr. Wayne Dyer, SARK, Louise Hay, and so many more... We explored many different types of trainings, including meditation.

I remember practicing meditation before it was an "in" thing. Back then, people did not openly share that they meditated. It was thought of like this thing that only strange people did while they sat in yoga poses, burned incense, and swayed side to side. The terms "life coach" and "self-help" were not common back then. In fact, the internet had not even been invented yet! 'lol.' It's crazy to think that my personal development journey got ignited that long ago.

Fast forward a few years later, in 1998, I produced and hosted a televised mind and body fitness show called *The Fitness Edge,* which aired on cable TV for over three years. I wanted to create something different that would inspire people to exercise and to take better care of their physical as well as mental health.

The show featured men and women of all ages, sizes, and fitness levels and had a special emphasis on tapping into the power of your mind to create the results you want. In addition to the workouts, I held interviews with people who had overcome odds and did not let life, nor their age, nor the events that had happened to them, hold them back.

Also, in the late 90s, I started writing health, fitness, and mental focus articles and was featured on the covers of local magazines and newspapers. My goal was to inspire people to realize that it's never too late to start over or to get your health back, or to re-train your brain to believe in the impossible.

In 2001, I started the first outdoor boot camp of its kind, called *The Fitness Edge Boot Camp*. I learned at a very young age that you will never stick to your fitness goals until you have the rest of your life in alignment. So, in addition to exercise and nutritional counseling, each participant was put through a life coaching course and given a workbook I had written called *"Get Out Of Your Way."*

The results were pretty impressive. My troopers were feeling so good about themselves and their transformations that they re-enlisted back into the program again and again. We had multiple troopers enlisted for nine and ten years! I eventually sold the boot camp and started a wellness company with a few business partners.

I was also a mind and body fitness speaker and got to travel and speak to different organizations. One of my favorite events was getting to be a speaker for the YPO's - The Young Presidents Organization while on an intimate, 180-person cruise that was traveling to 22 countries and seven continents. A few of our stops were Antarctica, New Zealand, Ushuaia Argentina, Punta Arenas Chile, and Easter Island Chile. Some of the guests on the ship and in the audience were Dan Aykroyd, Robert F. Kennedy Jr, Diana Krall, Art Garfunkel, and F.W. de Klerk (past president of South Africa). I remember Robert's wife, Mary, walking up to me after the event and gave me her number and said she wanted to learn more. I was floored! (Very surreal moment).

I am not telling you this story to impress you, I'm sharing this with you to impress upon you that visualization really works.

Once I figured out how to fine tune my visualization skills, I used it all the time. And there was this one day where I put on my list of goals that I wanted to meet someone who had overcome adversity and did it by the way of exercise. No joke - within just days it seemed, the goal manifested itself!

I was given the opportunity to meet Bob, "Mr. Inspiration" Wieland. Bob is a Vietnam war veteran who lost both legs to a mortar mine. Knowing that the Lord had a higher purpose and a bigger vision for him after the accident - he set out on a mission to accomplish things that were thought to be impossible!

He trained his body just as hard, if not harder than most seasoned athletes. He went on to break world records for bench pressing and entered marathons and triathlons. He also walked across America on his hands! It took him three years, eight months, and six days to complete the challenge across the US. These events helped launch him into one of the most sought after faith-based speakers.

I was so impressed with his story that I wrote an article about him. My article made the featured story for LA Fitness Magazine. Right after the magazine hit the shelves, both Bob and I were booked to speak in Hawaii for a wellness company. This was another goal that I had written down, and it manifested itself - in a matter of a few weeks!

The things you've just heard might sound nice and represent a foundation for my experience. But how is that going to help you? What you need to hear are the rough and edgy parts, the parts where I was at wits' end and didn't know how I was going to move on.

My life went on to take many twists and turns. On the outside, my life looked fun and exciting. I was really good at suppressing my fears, my anxiety, and hiding the pain I was going through for years and years. No one knew what I was going through. And because I held all those emotions inside for so many years, there was finally a tipping point to where I couldn't take it anymore.

It wasn't until four years ago that I took my deepest dive into personal transformation. That's when I finally became my true authentic self and faced my fears… and faced all those voices in my head that told me my best days were over.

You're about to learn how I reinvented my life, my career and created one heck of an Epic Encore!

If all I do is help one person, then all the blood, sweat, and tears that I went through in life will be well worth it.

We are all here for a reason, and it's up to us to figure out why our journeys take us where they do. And it's up to us to learn that in each event - good or bad, there is a grander lesson being taught.

What do we do with these lessons? Why do they happen? How can we use those lessons to help ourselves and to help others?

How do we find the strength to start over, or to be brave, or to try something new, or to go back to something we truly love or to find out what our purpose in life is all about?

I don't have all the answers to life, but I do know this - you are never too old to start over, and it's never too late to begin again. I am living proof that you can start over, pick up where you left off, or reinvent yourself at any age.

So, let's do this! Let us begin the journey to Your Epic Encore!

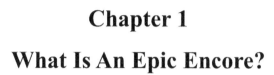

Chapter 1

What Is An Epic Encore?

To reinvent or transform yourself means letting go of emotions, past traumas, distractions, possessions, junk, and maybe even friends and family that are currently holding you back. It means letting go of old habits that no longer serve you. It means stepping away from routines, roles, and self-imposed responsibilities that have been pinning you down and keeping you from living life to its fullest.

You will finally be in the driver's seat, holding the wheel, and you will get to change the direction of your life.

It means making a new set of choices and paving new roads that lead to new opportunities, connections, and adventures.

Basically, you're giving yourself permission to start over and permission to have a great life!

We're not dead until we're dead! So why not start right now and make your remaining years your BEST years?

"No Matter How Hard The Past,
You Can Always Begin Again." — Buddha

In order to move forward in your life, one of the first steps you need to take is revisiting your past.

It's been proven that events that occur in your younger years, from birth to about ten years old, will dictate how you will handle just about every situation in your life for the rest of your life - good or bad.

Although our bodies will grow up and mature, the character traits and mentalities that were formed in response to a person or event in our childhood become our ingrained, imprinted templates for how we will interpret just about everything in the future. We'll cover more about this in Chapter 6.

When I was about seven years old, my parents divorced, and I thought they were divorcing because of me (I didn't know any better). And when they surprisingly got back together about two years later, I had already lost that bond with my dad (and did not get that bond back until my late teens).

I remember both of them working long hours, and my mom going back to college to be a nurse in her 40s. I also remember my parents having financial difficulties and going through bankruptcy. Although I grew up and became an adult, these two events (divorce and bankruptcy) made an imprint in my subconscious mind. I interpreted them to mean that money will always be tight and that the relationships in my life were going to be challenging. This theme continued throughout my life. I never figured out why until I took the time and effort to dive deep into self-reflection.

Also, it was not a normal thing to go back to college in your 40s back then, especially married women with children. It wasn't until years later that I appreciated what a feat this was for my mom and how hard she worked and studied. This woman is where I get a lot of my inner strength never to give up and that it's never too late to start over.

"Our Greatest Weakness Lies In Giving Up. The Most Certain Way To Succeed Is To Always Try Just One More Time."
— Thomas Edison

I was extremely shy in my early years, but luckily, my parents put me in something that brought me out of my shell: cheerleading. In the south, cheerleading is like a rite of passage. And in my local area, it was something every little girl wanted to do, and it was highly competitive.

I started cheering at nine years old and continued for about ten years. Some of my biggest life lessons were from being part of a team. We practiced our routines till we were utterly exhausted and aching with sprains, strains, bumps, bruises, and more. Blood, sweat, and tears were a daily thing. We were so dedicated and disciplined; we put numerous hours into training, and we were absolutely crushed and cried our hearts out when we didn't win at competitions.

It was hard to be a good sport about losing. We lost so many cheer competitions year after year. It really bothered me. I was compelled to do something about it, but I was so young. What could I possibly do to make a difference?

I was in this organization called Shelby Youth Sports, where you started at eight years old and could continue up to age twelve. At thirteen years old, I was too old to be in the program. So, I decided to come back the next year as a coach and choreographer. I loved it so much; I coached on and off for seven more years teaching teams in Tennessee as well as California.

But let's get back to my first team. It was my mission to do something with this cheer program to turn it around. The first and second years were dismal. We never won - not even third place. But in my third year of coaching, I started learning about visualization techniques. I would tell my cheerleaders to visualize the dance routine before they went on stage, and I would have them practice in their minds on the sidelines until they knew the routine by heart. I would have them see the trophy in their hands and the crowds cheering them on!

Then after three years of working with this organization, not only did we start winning competitions - but we beat the undefeated champions! The underdogs beat one of the best teams in the league! This was such a big deal. We made the news in the papers, and all of us were on cloud nine for months. This role as a coach gave me confidence beyond my wildest dreams. It taught me that anything is possible when you are consistent and do the work required. And the most important lesson I learned is you have to "want it" so strongly that nothing will knock you off track, no matter what life throws at you.

During my years of coaching, I was also cheering for Junior High and High School. Then, I went on to dance professionally as a "Dreamboat" for the Memphis Showboats USFL football team. And then I danced as a "Weathergirl" for the Memphis Storm soccer team for two years. I loved dancing but still did not know what I wanted to do career-wise.

After graduating from high school, I attended an art college on a scholarship for one year. I thought art was the right major because I loved drawing, and I loved being creative. But I just felt like there was something else out there for me. I thought switching colleges might help. So, I attended the main university in Memphis, TN, and after a few months, I dropped out. Suddenly, I was lost, and I didn't know what I wanted to do with my life. I felt like I had no clear direction for my future. So, I started focusing more on fashion show modeling and promotional modeling.

"The Pain You Feel Today Will Be
The Strength You Feel Tomorrow."
— Author Unknown

Then one pivotal night changed my life forever.

I was driving home from modeling in a late-night fashion show. I fell asleep at the wheel, and my car slammed into a light pole! The impact was so strong, the pressure bent the car frame and broke the light pole in half!

The windshield cracked into thousands of tiny pieces but did not break apart or fall down. However, there was a protrusion, a dome shape in the glass that stuck out about two or three inches.

It was the mold of my head when I hit the windshield on impact! I remember hearing the sound of the glass cracking and feeling my head whip back into the car seat with a ferocity. After that, I don't remember much.

There was an incredible amount of force as I got ejected towards the windshield - my body bent the steering wheel in half! And strangely, there was an impression of my teeth on the dashboard! This was before airbags were invented so you can imagine the impact.

I can't explain how I survived this car wreck. But I do know this - it is without a doubt a divine miracle that I'm alive today and did not suffer any broken bones or head injuries. I know I had angels, the Lord above, source, or whatever you want to call it - they were there looking over me. I was given the gift of life.

I have never taken that day for granted and often think back to that moment to remind myself that I was kept here for a reason. And I now know that reason is to do whatever I can to help others start over, pick up where they left off or to dream a new dream.

Being in this car accident forced me to wake up and take charge of my life.

However, it seemed like I had to keep re-learning this lesson throughout my life in different scenarios.

Chapter 2

Finding The Light In The Darkest Places

Have you ever had a gut feeling you shouldn't do something, but you do it anyway? Yep, that was me at 19 years old. A few months after the car wreck, I moved to Atlanta, GA, with a boyfriend I had been dating for a few years. Unfortunately, he would take steroids and have fits of rage. I knew this but still made the decision to move seven hours away from my family. I thought I could change him or that the move would make things better.

He and I would argue often, mostly about his outbursts when he was taking steroids. Like the time I came home from work and thought we had been robbed! Every drawer in the house was open and empty, and its contents were on the floor. And in the bedroom - the drawers had been yanked out and thrown around the room. When I asked him about this, his reply was simply, "Oh, I couldn't find my hairbrush."

I knew his temper was getting out of control, but I was afraid of what he might do if I told him I wanted to break up. Then, one day we were about to leave the house, and he demanded that I change the jeans I was wearing (even though they were ok to wear the day before when we were at the movies). When I said that I wasn't going to change and walked towards the bathroom, he pushed me inside the walk-in closet and blocked the exit. When I tried to get around him, he punched me so hard in the stomach that it knocked the breath out of me, and I fell backward, knocking the clothes off their hangers one by one.

That was the moment that ended the relationship. Being in that wreck made me realize I am here for a much bigger reason, and if I stayed with him, I would probably never live my life to its fullest potential. So, I got the courage to leave him and moved to Raleigh, North Carolina, where my parents had just moved. Truth be told, I could not have done it without their help.

Although I loved them dearly, having to move back in with my parents was absolutely deflating. I felt like I had failed. It took everything I had to get over the break-up with my boyfriend and the embarrassment of living with my parents again. Back then, in my circle of friends, no one moved back home with their parents after moving out!

After a few weeks of self-pity - I dug in deep and decided that I needed to make a change and that I was the only thing holding me back from having the life I wanted.

"New Beginnings Are Often Disguised As Painful Endings."
- Lao Tzu

Shortly after moving back in with my parents, I started working in an upscale retail clothing store in the mall. I love clothes; I love the mall, easy job, right? Wrong. I never had a consistent schedule and could never plan anything in advance. I spent every paycheck on clothes from the store and was constantly written up for closing the cash drawer wrong at night or wearing the wrong shoes, etc. (according to the General Manager).

Then, one day I was making a clothing display on the wall with a fellow employee. We were discussing how we felt about working in this store. Then she said to me, "you know, if we had any sense, we would pack our things and move to Myrtle Beach, South Carolina." I had no idea where that was, but all I heard was "beach," and I said, "let's do it!" So after about only three months in North Carolina, I moved to Myrtle Beach, South Carolina, which was a little over three hours away from my parents.

My friend and I were only twenty years old and barely had about $200 each to our name. We rented a room in a beach house that was built up on stilts. It was a run-down old house managed by this older woman who rummaged through all the rooms when all the renters were away. She stole our toaster and curling iron! Why she needed those two items, we'll never know! But we saw her walking through the central courtyard with them in her hands! Every day we wondered what would be missing next when we got back to our creepy room!

We shared a bathroom with whoever was renting the room next to us. It was one of those Jack and Jill bathrooms where you have to remember to lock and unlock the door for the other renter. It was so scary! The keys to the doors were those old, antique, skeleton keys that barely worked. The floors creaked every time we took one step. There was no kitchenette or mini-fridge - just a bed, a dresser, and our toaster and curling iron (that we really missed)! We were struggling and did whatever we could to make our money go further - including eating peanut butter and jelly sandwiches every day as well as having to share the same bed. We didn't care. We were going to do whatever we could to make it on our own.

Fast forward a couple of months, through one of her connections - she got a job managing a retail store, and I got a job managing a party supply shop. After some time, we saved up enough money to move out of the creepy house, and we rented a condo on the beach!

And just when we thought we had it made and things were turning around for us, we were told to evacuate! Hurricane Hugo was coming towards our beaches, and it plowed through our town with a massive fury! It destroyed homes and buildings all over Myrtle Beach, including the condo we had just moved into five days earlier! Yep, you heard that right, we got to enjoy the condo for a whopping 5 days!

So, it was back to square one again for us! After a few weeks, we eventually found a new place to live a few blocks from the beach. And a few months later, we got settled into our new routines as two, young, independent women. I was so happy and thought I was "living the life" in a beach town while making about $275 a week! It's crazy how far I could make that little bit of money go back then.

Unfortunately, that adventure was also short-lived. The party store I managed closed after about two years. I had a staff of employees, and I felt terrible when I had to give them the news we were closing. This event really devastated me.

Again, here I was back to square one and in another situation where I had no idea what I was going to do or how I would be able to make ends meet. Work was really hard to find. Most jobs were in the hotel, restaurant, or night club business. And they all closed during the winter because, at that time, tourists only visited Myrtle Beach during the spring and summer months.

Prior to the party store closing, I had been meeting all these great people in town and helping them with their party supplies and giving them ideas on how to decorate their events, etc. And then one day - it hit me. Maybe I could open a party decorating business and service all these businesses that had been shopping in our store. So, I opened up *"Party Perfect"* decorating services. I was the only employee, and sometimes decorating an event would take me all day, but I absolutely loved it! I didn't make that much money, but I was my own boss. This is where I first learned the long, hard road about being an entrepreneur.

Although the beach life was fun, living in a tourist town was not easy. People would come and go so quickly. Men were fickle as ever; they had an endless supply of girls in bikinis on every beachfront. Needless to say, I had a string of boyfriends... The alcoholic chef, the non-committal shop owner, the Casanova actor, the sweetest pot-smoking-bible-thumper, and the born-again Christian who broke up with me (two weeks before he was going to propose). How did I know he was going to propose? This guy made plans to make plans and told me in advance he was going to propose to me at a certain time in a certain town. Ha!

All the while, I knew I wanted more out of life and my career, but never demanded more out of the men in my life. I just accepted things as is. I never grasped or understood my true value and continued to make not so great choices in men according to those not so great values.

"The Most Important Thing In Life Is To Stop Saying 'I wish' And Start Saying 'I Will.' Consider Nothing Impossible, Then Treat Possibilities As Probabilities."
— Charles Dickens

While running the party decorating business, I also was doing promotional modeling. I worked events as a promo model, and sometimes I would be the event manager. Then, one day the moon and the stars aligned, and I was presented an opportunity to work for an event management company in Los Angeles. I got that "calling," you know, that one where if you don't follow or listen to it, you know you will regret it for the rest of your life?

So, in 1994, I moved by myself from one coast to the other - from Myrtle Beach, SC to Belmont Shore, CA. It was just a few months after the Northridge earthquake. But I did not let that stop me! Everyone thought I was crazy for moving alone, and so far away! I had my eyes set on my goal, and nothing was going to get in my way.

Shortly after moving to Los Angeles, what did I do after finding a great guy? I was so focused on my career that I pushed him away, and that relationship ended after two years!
Then, one day while working a promotional event, I met this very interesting man. My alarm bells were going off left and right. My gut was telling me to walk away, but I did not listen.

He reeled me in with his humor which made me want to get to know him more. He asked if he could take me on a date that following weekend. I declined because I was traveling for work and wouldn't be able to go out for a few weeks. It ended up being about three months before we had our first date in the spring. And the days that passed after that first date, he seemed fine. In fact, he seemed like Mr. Wonderful! We had so much fun together, and his kids were amazing. Each date was better than the one before, so my initial concerns went away.

We lived over an hour apart, and the drive was starting to wear on both of us. So when he asked me to move in with him just months later that summer, I didn't think twice. I threw caution to the wind and moved in with him and his two kids!

Right after I moved in, he was charismatic, funny, and a blast to be around. But after a few months, I started seeing this other side of him. He was a full-blown, Dr. Jeckyll and Mr. Hyde, yelling, screaming, threatening, and sometimes hitting his sons and me.

He had moments where he could be nice. I remember him making dinner with some cool cocktails, a nice fire in the outdoor fire pit, and relaxing music playing. But all it would take is for one little thing to ruin the whole night. It might be we were out of cherries for the cocktails. It might be the speaker playing music outdoors was full of static. It could be the dog walked up and sniffed the table. I never knew when the bomb was going to go off. I could never predict what was going to cause him to explode.

Some days he'd be giving me lavish gifts like a beautiful fur coat (which I did not want nor did I ask for) while on vacation in Alaska. And then the next vacation, he'd be threatening me in a whispering voice at the back of my neck, saying, "You're lucky the kids are with us, or I'd push you off the back of this ship. No one would ever know, and you'd never be found." To the people standing nearby, they probably thought he was whispering sweet nothings in my ear while we were looking towards the sunset. In reality, I was gripping the railing on the ship while fearing for my life.

Many times in his fits of rage, he would hit me with an object. One day it might be with a video camera or one of those long steering wheel locks. And the next day, it might be with a book. Basically, it was anything nearby that he could get his hands on fast enough as he was exploding.

Well, on this one day in particular - he used his fist. He went to punch me in the face, and I turned my head. His punch landed so hard on my ear; he ruptured my eardrum. I was in so much pain; I fell to the floor. I went to the emergency care to get it looked at, and the doctor questioned me. The doctor knew I did not "fall and hit the doorknob," as I told him. He then asked a few other questions and said he had to call the police by law. This event happened right after the OJ trial. So, any hint of domestic violence - the police would show up at the residence, ask a few questions to the boyfriend or spouse, and off to jail, they would go.

My boyfriend called me from jail and pleaded with me to change my story to the investigator, and regretfully, I did. They released him the very next day. And sure enough, he went right back to his old habits. I knew that I should not have changed my story on what happened, but I was afraid of what he would do to me after he got out of jail.

Right about now, you're probably wondering why in the world would I let anyone treat me like that? Why wouldn't I just leave? It's hard for those who've never been with an abusive person to fathom putting up with this. For those who have been in abusive situations for any length of time, you know precisely why it was hard to leave. There was so much mental abuse that I started to lose "me." I began to believe all the things he told me, such as I was ugly, fat, old, stupid, would never make it on my own, and the list goes on.

I wanted to run away so many times, but I couldn't leave these innocent kids who were learning all the wrong ways to be a man. I helped raise these boys for eight years. I did whatever I could to let them know, their father's actions were not normal. And that a good man would never treat the woman he loves or his kids this way.

After so many years of this abuse, it got to a point where I had lost all hope. He had me so trapped in my own mental jail, and I couldn't see a way out. There were multiple days I wanted to die, I wanted him to just kill me (like he threatened to do numerous times), or I was going to end my life myself. I didn't care anymore. You can only be yelled at and abused so many times before you just want to give up.

"Never Regret A Day In Your Life: Good Days Give Happiness, Bad Days Give Experience, Worst Days Give Lessons, And Best Days Give Memories." — Unknown

---

I even went to the local domestic violence center to get help. I couldn't let anyone know. In fact, no one knew what I had been through, not even my family. If my boyfriend found out that I went to the center, he would have had screamed and threatened me till he was blue in the face. He was so worried about his image and was so afraid others would find out that he's not the "Mr. Wonderful" that he was portraying to the outside world.

So, I used a fake name, wore a hat and glasses and no make-up. I walked into the center, sat down, and my heart sank. "What's that on the coffee table in front of me? It's me on the cover of a local magazine! Crap, now I really can't say anything!" So, I flipped the magazine over and listened to the advice the facilitator was giving and did not reveal what I was really going through.

But deep down inside - I truly wanted to tell it all. I was praying for a miracle. I was hoping someone or any one of my friends would find out and say "We know you're being abused, we're going to help you pack up your things and get you out of there." But I just was afraid of what he might do. So, I kept my dreams of breaking away stuffed deep down inside for a few more years.

What's crazy is that he was in the self-help field! He had a library of self-help cassettes that he sold online. He helped many people overcome all kinds of issues, but he couldn't help himself. And this was during the time I was also in the self-help field! I was a mind and body fitness speaker and had started my Fitness TV show and had launched the life coaching program with my fitness boot camp members!

On the outside, I looked like I had my act together and had this dream life of exciting travel around the world. However, on the inside, I was living a life of hell at home, then waking up at four am to be the motivator for all these amazing people who had joined my outdoor boot camp! I could never let them know what I was going through. I had to be strong and courageous for them and lift them up every day.

For years and years, I prayed, begged, pleaded, and cried for an answer on how to break free from him. It was not until after eight excruciating years that I was finally able to get out of this abusive relationship. I'll share more on that at another time.

If you need help getting out of an abusive situation please know there is help available. There are resources in the back of this book or feel free to reach out to me.

Chapter 3

Epic Speed Bumps & Reinventions

I will never forget this moment. I was sitting in one of the small consultation rooms at the doctor's office. It was in 2009. "Are you sure you're looking at my records?" I asked the doctor. "Yes, these are your results," she said. I could not believe she diagnosed me with having advanced arthritis and told me that I needed both knees replaced!

I thought, "How was this possible? I ate healthier than anyone and worked out all the time. Did all those years of dance catch up with me? Did the car wreck catch up with me? What did I do wrong? What should I have done differently?" The doctor told me to stop everything that I was doing and get used to having pain for the rest of my life (unless I had this surgery). She made me feel like an old horse that needed to be put out to the pasture to die!

After going into a deep depression for some time with the pain and the stiffness, I finally shifted my thoughts and realized the doctors' diagnosis was a gift. I honestly thought, "Ok, if I am really falling apart like you say I am, then I guess I better get on with living my life to its fullest! I can't waste any more time!"

The doctor's diagnosis was like a spark plug that ignited my drive to do something crazy and epic. It was if I wanted to prove the doctor wrong. I wanted to prove that I was still vibrant and thriving (contrary to what she told me).

I decided to make a list of all the things that one with arthritis should not be able to do. And Aerial fitness was one of those things on my list. I had wanted to do this for so many years, but every time I looked up aerial fitness online, the schools were only for advanced athletes and Russian gymnasts who practically popped out of the womb doing backflips!

So, I just kept visualizing and seeing myself up in the air and climbing on these silks. I didn't know how it was going to happen. I just knew it WAS going to happen. I didn't even know what the apparatus was called! I Googled "curtains, ribbons, fabric," etc. I eventually discovered they were called silks or tissu (without the "e"). So, I looked high and low, and after months of searching - I found an awesome little studio that was open to everyday people like me (someone who is not a teenage Russian gymnast)! Ha!

"Some People Succeed Because They Are Destined To, But Most People Succeed Because They Are Determined To." — Unknown

---

At first, I thought, "What the heck was I thinking? This is the hardest workout I have ever encountered!" I was the oldest student in every class, and even just the most basic moves were hard for me. But I did not give up. I just kept coming back and training more and more. I went every week for two times a week, for two years. I got stronger, more flexible, more confident, and the list goes on and on. I was on top of the world! I was in my 40s performing aerial stunts alongside students more than half my age!

After a couple of years, I started teaching and performing in aerial! It's been ten years since my first class. I have now performed over lakes, between mountain peaks, in front of waterfalls, over swimming pools, and so much more. It has changed my life; I can do things now in my 50s that I couldn't even dream of doing in my 20s - even the splits!

I couldn't believe it! I finally found something that made me feel alive and helped re-invent myself... And now, I send out gratitude to that doctor who told me I couldn't all those years ago.

I never had the knee surgery and instead changed my food intake, and I found some amazing supplements that made a profound change with my joint pain. (See the back of the book for more info).

Knowing that I could not do the high impact workouts anymore with my arthritis, I sold the boot camp, and I started a health and wellness company with a couple of business partners. Little did we know, the market crash was coming. Companies were closing left and right, but we opened during this transitional time.

Within the first year, a well-known national health store chain offered to buy us out for over 1.5 million. But we declined, we had a bigger vision and bigger dreams. We were very different, and we knew they would change our concept. We purposely only sold to mom and pop stores so we could help the small business owner stay alive (by carrying a product that customers could only get at their store).

Unfortunately, after about ten years, I was let go. The company I helped build, the company that I worked so many hours on that I sacrificed getting married and having kids - all of that went out the window. I kept thinking my dedication would pay off. I did everything from cleaning the toilets to print marketing, writing articles, digital marketing to creating artwork, designing the website, helping customers online and in the store, and so much more.

If losing my career was not bad enough, it was also around this time that my boyfriend and I broke up. I spent months in yet another deep depression trying to figure out what I was going to do.

I was riddled with questions. "Who wants to hire someone my age? What value am I to anyone? I have advanced arthritis - I can't start another boot camp - it's too hard on my body! Who wants to date me? Men my age want women half their age! Where do I go from here?"

"When One Door Closes, Another One Opens:
But We Often Look So Long And Regretfully Upon The
Closed Door That We Do Not See The One Which
Has Opened For Us." — Alexander Graham Bell

Every day I would listen to motivating speeches on Youtube to get some kind of spark started. I would listen to comedians to try to cheer myself up. I would meditate, I would pray, I would listen to faith-based sermons, I would journal, I would read motivational books, I would spend time with friends. These things were helping temporarily, but nothing was sticking.

On the outside - I looked like everything was fine. I did not let anyone know what I was going through, although they probably saw it in my eyes and by me gaining about 15 pounds. On the inside, I was crumbling. I didn't want to get out of bed; I had no energy. All I wanted to do was eat bad food, not exercise, watch TV all day, and feel sorry for myself.

I kept thinking, "How did this become my life? I was supposed to be married for 20 or more years by now. I should've had kids by now. I should be planning to retire soon and watching grandkids grow up. How did this happen to me? Why am I having to start over? How do I start over again? This isn't fair!"

Yep, that was me just a few years ago. I was mentally stuck in my old "story." I had yet to clearly see the "gift" in the events that had happened to me. My thoughts were muddy, and I was spinning my wheels in victim mode. Little did I know, everything was about to change in ways I could have never predicted.

Chapter 4

Finding The Needle In The Hay Stack

And then, one day, it finally happened. I found a much sought-after mentor and worth every dime! In fact, I found a group of mentors and a program that completely changed my life! I went in thinking I was going to learn how to start an online business and ended up also going through a series of self-development courses. I was surrounded by a positive new group of fellow entrepreneurs, business owners, thought shakers, and out of the box explorers who all were taking massive action in their lives.

Before I started these courses and studying with these different mentors, I kept thinking, "But I've been a life coach before, I was a motivational speaker before. I've read so many books and bought so many programs on how to improve one's life. I know all the jargon and mental tricks you are supposed to use to snap yourself out of it. How is this going to be any different?"

But something was VERY different in these courses that I attended. I learned how to get to the root of what was eating away at me. I learned how to diffuse the negative charge I had placed on each of the events that had happened to me. I learned how to completely surrender and be one hundred percent real and authentic. I discovered that laying all my cards out on the table and facing my circumstances head-on was one of the most freeing experiences ever.

"The Only Person You Are Destined To Become
Is The Person You Decide To Be."
— Ralph Waldo Emerson

After an intensive, four-year deep dive into personal and business development and investing over 70K in my education, I found myself! I discovered my "why." I got my voice, my light, and my reason for living back. I started attracting new opportunities. I opened two new businesses. I attracted the most wonderful, handsome man into my life, and get this – he's younger than me! And he is one hundred percent supportive with my endeavors and he is by far the greatest cheerleader of my life!

I finally had this epiphany… I realized that the car wreck, dropping out of college, the abusive boyfriends, the break ups, the dead-end jobs, losing my career, and all the trials and tribulations I had been through in my life was so that I could experience life's greatest lessons. And it was up to me to find the "gift" or the blessing in each event and then use these lessons to help others.

Cherie Carter-Scott, Ph.D. sums it best in her book - *10 Rules for Being Human.* She explains that there are no mistakes - only lessons and those lessons will keep getting repeated until you have learned the lesson.

Oh, great, right?! Well, not to worry! The good news is what you make of your life is up to YOU.

You already have all the answers inside of you. All you need to do is trust the process and find the right method that resonates with your heart and soul.

So, if you're having one of those days, months, years, etc. where you know there is something better out there for you - you're right!

And if you're reading this book and you've made it this far - then you're ready to start the process. I am so excited to see you grow, to see the doors of life open for you and to hear all the great stories of how you created ***Your Epic Encore!***

After all the years of speed bumps, auto-corrections, and more, I figured out which techniques were the most instrumental in making important changes in my life as well as the lives of my clients.

I discovered that there are 9 Pillars to reinvention:

I.   **Find Your Point A & Point B**
II.   **Retrain Your Brain**
III.   **Revisit The Past**
IV.   **Forgive Yourself and Others**
V.   **Visualize Your Future**
VI.   **Affirm Your Worth**
VII.   **Be Grateful For Everything**
VIII.   **Get Grounded in Meditation**
IX.   **Find a Mentor**

We will cover these nine pillars in the following chapters.

Please know I am not a doctor, a psychologist, nor a therapist, and these techniques are not intended to cure or treat any disease. I am just sharing with you some of the things that I have learned and applied over the past twenty years with the hopes that it will help you as it has helped me.

Pillar I

What's Your Point A
& Point B?

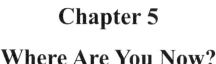

Chapter 5

Where Are You Now?

By now, hopefully, you believe me when I say, "just trust me, I've been there!"

All of us encounter setbacks. All of us go through ups and downs. It's how we react to those situations that make all the difference.

Time is the most precious commodity that you can never get back. Are you going to stay knocked down, or are you going to get up, dust yourself off and plot a new course?

Let's face the facts:

You will not take action unless you are motivated or inspired to do so. And most of us will not make changes until we are completely uncomfortable, fed up, sick and tired of being sick and tired, frazzled, and frustrated.

In other words, you must decide right now that you are the most important thing in this equation. You must choose yourself. If not now, when are you finally going to put YOU first?

Look at what needs changing or improving. You must feel the pain or discomfort strong enough to make significant, long-lasting changes in your life. You must peel back the layers and honestly look at where you are right now and how you got here...

"When I Let Go Of What I Am, I Become What I
Might Be. When I Let Go Of What I Have,
I Receive What I Need." — Lao Tzu

Every problem we have with our health, stress levels, anxiety, our careers, our families, our relationships, etc., there is a layer underneath that you must shine a light on so you can heal it and send it on its way.

Decide Where You Are At Right Now...
What Is Your Point A?

Then Decide, What Is Your Point B?
What's The Outcome You Want To Achieve?

Why are you reading this book?

Is there any part of your life you would like to change or improve?

Do you want to reinvent yourself? Are you craving Your Epic Encore?

Are you wanting to discover your life's purpose, enhance potential, and develop strengths or talents?

Do you want to grow your business and or career? Or attain a goal that seems out of reach?

Have you been living your life for everyone else for so many years, and now you want to live life for you?

Do you have the life of your dreams already but want something more?

Do you want to create or build something so you can leave a legacy behind (that helps others)?
Have you gained or lost weight and have been letting your health deteriorate because you've been so focused on work or taking care of others first?

Have you been stuck at the same job for years but are afraid to leave? Maybe you have a fear of not finding anything better? Fear of losing benefits? Fear of what the family will say?

Have you lost a loved one and have been mourning their passing for so long, you have lost sight of your needs and desires?

Did you start a company and were once so passionate about it, but now you can't stand it? It causes you so much stress and anxiety, and now you want out?

Are you divorced or out of a relationship, and now you want to start over?

Are you a cancer survivor, and now you are ready to take on the world, living each day to its fullest?

Were you in an abusive or strained relationship with a loved one or family member and were never allowed to grow or do things without approval?

Did you survive a serious accident or near-death experience and realized you were going through the motions of life before, but now you want to get every last drop of excitement out of life?

Do you spend your days thinking there has got to be something better out there for you, but you don't know how to get started?

Do you want to develop self-confidence or to grow spiritually or enhance your quality of life?

Are you having a hard time making ends meet and or are in debt up to your eyeballs - but don't know how to stop the cycle?
Are you stressed out daily and rarely spend time with family because you are so focused on work or other issues?

Have you spent your life seeking the approval of friends, family members, or your spouse for every move you make? But now you're ready to learn how to grab life by the horns on your own?

Have you been playing small, trying not to stand out too much, or call too much attention to yourself? But now you're ready to bust out and have the best life ever?

Are you living a life on the outside where everyone thinks you are fine, but deep down inside, you are falling apart?

Maybe you are being abused and can't tell anyone. Maybe your spouse or boyfriend/girlfriend puts on an act on the outside world - but behind closed doors, they take out their anger or frustrations on you.

Are you tired of attracting all the wrong people into your life and can't figure out how to stop the cycle?

Did you wake up one day and realize, "I've wasted so much time! Where did my life go?"

Let's set the course for your future.

Write your answers below. If you need to keep your answers private, put your answers in another place.

Whatever you do - don't cheat yourself out of getting the full benefits. Do the excavating... Let's dig deep! Now use your own words.

What is your point A? Where are you starting from today? Where are you right now?

POINT A:

_____

_____

_____

_____

_____

_____

_____

_____

_____

_____

_____

_____

_____

_____

What is your point B? Where do you want to go?
What's the outcome you want to achieve?

POINT B:

_____

_____

_____

_____

_____

_____

_____

_____

_____

_____

_____

_____

_____

As we move through each chapter, you will have multiple opportunities to work on these answers.

Pillar II

Retrain The Brain

Chapter 6

Subconscious Powerhouse

You know the excitement you get when you want to try something new, but then you start feeling all tense and anxious? That's your subconscious mind trying to pull you back to your comfort zone.

To reinvent yourself, or to have Your Epic Encore, you must be willing to embrace that feeling of being uncomfortable when trying new things.

And the first step is to begin by changing your thoughts, actions, and habits.

In order to do this, we need to talk about your mental powerhouse - your subconscious mind. The subconscious mind is much more powerful at processing information than the conscious mind. The subconscious accounts for about 95% of your brain, while the conscious is about 5%.

The subconscious mind is your internal computer and memory bank for every experience you've had. It permanently stores everything that has ever happened to you and everything that you have observed - especially in your developmental years. And the things that were negative or on the more traumatic side, your subconscious mind holds onto those like glue.

A few examples are: like when you broke your moms' favorite dish and she yelled at you, when your parents got a divorce, and you felt deserted, when your uncle was fired from his job and he lost his ambition to do anything else, when your friend broke their ankle and they never played sports again, when you were bullied at school and felt like no one liked you, when your teacher scolded you and told you that you would never go anywhere in life, when your parents didn't show up for an event at school and you felt unimportant, etc.

"Reality Is Created By The Mind. We Can Change Our Reality By Changing Our Mind." — Plato

---

Believe it or not, events do not cause positive or negative feelings. We create these feelings ourselves based on how we interpret each event.

The subconscious mind only knows what you tell it. It does not know right from wrong or good from the bad. It's where you make most of your decisions, and it's where we tend to get stuck.

Your subconscious stores your perceptions, reactions, beliefs, patterns, habits, and emotions, etc. Although our bodies grow up and mature, the character traits and mentalities formed in response to a person or event in our childhood become our downloaded programs - even if they are disempowering or self-sabotaging.

The amygdala is one of two almond-shaped masses of nuclei located deep in the temporal lobe. It is responsible for the fight-or-flight response that causes you to respond to threats. The amygdala forms connections to specific events and starts substantially reinforcing those experiences.

Your amygdala quickly searches your database for a time this event or a similar situation occurred in your life. It finds something close and sends out signals to the body to respond. Basically, your amygdala makes mountains out of molehills. The amygdala shuts down the neural pathway to your prefrontal cortex, and all rational thinking goes out the window.

Ever caught yourself or witnessed someone over-reacting to the simplest thing as if it was life-threatening? I sure have! Remember the short-tempered boyfriends I mentioned earlier? I witnessed two grown men having melt-downs like a child for over ten years! But at least now I understand them a little better.

This reaction is also known as amygdala hijacking, a term coined by author Daniel Goleman of ***Emotional Intelligence***. This happens before the conscious mind even has an opportunity to become aware. And once a strong emotion has been turned on, the conscious mind has trouble turning it off. Your system is flooded with adrenaline and cortisol, causing an increased heart rate, sweaty palms, and shallow breathing.

This response can be triggered by the simplest things like someone cutting in line or a stranger spilling a drink on you. Then, you start yelling at the other person and making a scene, only to realize later that you were overreacting after you calmed down.

How do we calm the mind in a situation like this? First of all - just breathe. Take a deep breath in as you count to five, and then exhale counting to five. Keep repeating until you feel a sense of calm coming over you. Then let go of the story on who is right or who is wrong or what really happened.

Just be present in the moment and practice gratitude. What did you learn from this event? How will you respond differently next time? Was this event really that bad? Having a daily mediation practice will also change your reactions and your outlook on life. We'll cover more on this in the upcoming chapters.

Your mind can be re-wired to help you achieve the desired change you're after. Situations, events, and other things that used to cause you anxiety or an adverse reaction can be replaced with a state of calm and feelings of gratitude and appreciation.

Here are a few methods that have worked best with my clients:

- Clarify: What do you really want to be, do, or have?
- Evaluate: What do you need to do to produce real, long-term change?
- Pinpoint: What is your built-in resistance to the changes you are making?

- Master: Replace negative emotional responses with more appropriate behaviors that are aligned with what you want.
- Initiate: Take daily steps and actions that are in alignment with your goals, wishes, and desires until they become your new daily habits.

Most of us know at least some of the things we need to do to be successful in the ways we have defined. The difference is you must be willing to do what it takes to achieve your goals and handle what life throws at you every day - even on those bad days, good days, sick days, vacation days, etc.

This type of self-discipline generates momentum after a while. The more you do each of these things, the more they align the subconscious mind with your conscious goals. This, in turn, automatically drives actions that are consistent with the vision you have, and changes occur easier and faster. We will dive deeper into this topic in the upcoming chapters.

Pillar III

Revisit The Past

Chapter 7

How Did You Get Here?

You have learned by now that we are creatures of habit and love staying nice and cozy in our comfort zones. And most of us will not take any consistent, massive action until we are just about at wit's end.

I love it when my clients say they are fed up! I love it when they say they can't take it anymore. Then, I know they are ready to take immense action.

So, let's dive in…

Are you happy with where you are right now? If things are fantastic, then great! What are you going to do to keep that great flow going? Especially when and if "life happens" and tries to knock you off course in the future?

Or, if you know some areas that could use some improvement or better yet - need drastic changes - then great!

Listen up! Get brutally honest with yourself.

There is only one of you... You only get one go at this life...

You are the only one that has the power to change your thoughts, your actions, and your outcomes. You are the one that gets to create and plan out *Your Epic Encore!*

"In The End, Only Three Things Matter:
How Much You Loved, How Gently You Lived,
And How Gracefully You Let Go Of Things
Not Meant For You." — Buddha

Stop waiting to be rescued and for someone to fix your problems. Stop waiting for the holidays to be over, or after summer vacation is over, or after school is out, or when the kids go to school or move out of the house, etc. Stop doing the same old things that weren't working before, but expecting a different outcome now.

Now is the time to take action. So, let's go through a series of self-discovery questions.

By answering the following questions, you will start to pinpoint things in your past or present that represent wins or losses, strengths or weaknesses, and how they impact your life today.

When it comes to your mission or your purpose in life, what is most important to you and why?

_____

_____

_____

Who are the most important people in your life, and what do they provide you with?

_____

_____

_____

Name one of your greatest successes in life up to today.

_____

_____

_____

Why is/was this success important to you?

_____

_____

_____

What was the mindset that dominated your thoughts when you were having success, and things were going great?

_____

_____

_____

Is that success still going? If not, then why not?

_____

_____

_____

What do you need to do to get it back?

_____

_____

_____

Name one of the biggest challenges you have faced in your life.

_____

_____

_____

How did you overcome it?

_____

_____

_____

If you have not overcome this challenge yet, then why not?

_____

_____

_____

What do you need to do to get over this challenge?

_____

_____

_____

What will happen if you do not get over this challenge?

_____

_____

_____

What is the one thing you are most afraid of?

_____

_____

_____

Why are you afraid of this one thing?

_____

_____

_____

If you conquered this one thing, what would it do for you?

_____

_____

_____

What are the things you know you must change?

_____

_____

_____

What do you think will happen if you do not make these changes?

_____

_____

_____

What do you think will happen if you do make these changes?

_____

_____

_____

You will soon discover in the upcoming chapter how your successes, and your challenges (or perceived challenges), are actually serving you.

Pillar IV

Forgive Yourself
& Others

Chapter 8

Set Yourself Free

Are you ready to forgive?

Forgiveness is a gift for your soul. Forgiving doesn't mean excusing or forgetting what happened. Forgiveness is something you do to lower your psychological distress by getting rid of those negative emotions. Studies have shown that more forgiving people are happier, more hopeful, and live longer.

We often think that if we keep this anger or resentment in our hearts, then we will be protecting ourselves from getting hurt again. However, every time you dwell on the pain from the past, you are allowing that situation or event to re-surface again and again in your present world. This negative vibration never goes away. It's like a storm cloud that hovers over your head and follows you around... for the rest of your life.

"The Weak Can Never Forgive. Forgiveness Is The Attribute Of The Strong." — Mahatma Gandhi

Forgiveness also applies to you personally. You must forgive yourself for the wrong turns you've made, the bad judgments you've had, the heated words you've spoken and or even the words that you think you should have said, or the actions you think you should have taken, etc. You must set yourself free and stop persecuting yourself.

Many times, we can not move forward in life because we are not happy with ourselves. Deep down inside, we do not love ourselves. We have never forgiven ourselves for something we have done or have never forgiven the thing or person that has hurt us. We stay trapped in this time warp repeating the same "mistakes," same thoughts, same words and same habits over and over.

What would happen if you finally had self-love or expressed self-love? If you don't take steps to forgive, you will internalize that pain and use that situation as the litmus test every time you have to make a decision.

Have you heard your internal dialogue saying any of the following?

"This person said they loved me, but yet they betrayed me. So, I will never trust another lover again."

"I have never been consistent with eating healthy and exercising, so I know I'm going to fail on this next diet as well."

"I invested all my hard-earned savings into something that turned into a flop. I will never trust my judgment to invest again."

"I made some bad judgments and decisions years ago and it still bothers me today."

And so on…. However, when you truly forgive, you let go of the negative emotions that pop up each time you think of that person or event. Without these negative charges or emotions, our stress levels decline, which in turn helps our body and our cells heal in multiple ways. Plus, you'll stop attracting negative situations or things in your life that prevent you from getting what you want.

If you can find the gift or blessing in the event(s) that have hurt you, held you back, changed your life, etc. you will set yourself free. Ask yourself: "How has this event or tragedy helped me? How did I get stronger? How did it help me grow? What new things did I try because of this event?"

Now, I know this thought process is not easy. In fact, I had a client who refused to do it. When Marie came to me, she was recently out of work and had gone through a divorce five years earlier. She said she felt stuck, had little to no motivation to strive for anything, and slept most of the day.

In the beginning, she was motivated by our talks and the progress she was making. But weeks later, she fell back into her old habits and lost her momentum.

After digging deeper, I discovered she was holding onto anger from the divorce and how it ended. And whenever I would start talking to her about forgiveness, she couldn't do the work. So I asked her a few things:

"How long have you been holding onto this resentment? Months? Years? How's that working out for you? What benefit are you getting from holding onto this anger or resentment? There must be some benefit, or you wouldn't still be attached to it. Are you getting special treatment from others because of what happened to you? How many times have you told this story to yourself or someone else? Are you using this story as an excuse to stop trying or to give up, or not to make a change? How is holding yourself back punishing the person who hurt you? That's like drinking poison but expecting the other person to get sick."

It was that day and that exact conversation that turned things around for her. She finally realized that holding onto her story was like a ten-ton weight dragging her down and keeping her from moving forward. When she dropped the "story," that meant she could no longer complain about being mistreated. That also meant it was time for her to grab the wheel and take control of her life.

Maybe you know someone like this. Perhaps, this person is you?

So, I'll say it again. It's time to forgive and to find the gifts or blessings. Take a moment and think through the following questions before answering.

Name one person, event, or thing you want to let go or to forgive from your past or present that will make you feel liberated?

_____

_____

_____

What are the benefits of letting go or forgiving this person, event, or thing from your past or present?

_____

_____

_____

What are the disadvantages of not letting go or forgiving this person, event, or thing from your past or present?

_____

_____

_____

Name one thing you want to forgive yourself for that will make you feel liberated?

_____

_____

_____

What are the benefits of letting go or forgiving yourself for this one thing?

_____

_____

_____

What are the disadvantages of not forgiving yourself for this one thing?

_____

_____

_____

Name one thing that is currently holding you back or causing you to feel stuck?

_____

_____

_____

Why do you let this programming hold you back?

_____

_____

_____

Where did you get that programming? From a spouse? Family
member? Teacher? Your own beliefs, etc.?

_____

_____

_____

What do you need to do to change that programming?

_____

_____

_____

Some pretty amazing things happen when you start being honest about
how you feel, what you want, and where you want to go. If you want to
change your future - you have to change the way you think. If the things
that keep showing up in your life are stressful and unhappy - then it's
time to try something different.

Stop worrying about what others think. Most people aren't thinking
about you, anyway. They are dealing with their own problems and
trying to figure out their own lives.

This next exercise is one that you will want to ponder on for a few minutes. Make sure you are being completely open and honest.
So, get real with yourself and answer this statement.

The Story That I Have Been Telling Myself For Years On

Why I Can't GET - BE - DO - or HAVE What I Want Is:

_____

_____

_____

_____

_____

_____

_____

_____

_____

_____

_____

_____

_____

_____

Let go of those burdens that have been weighing you down.

Now is the time to stop walking around repeating that same old story of why you can't get, be, do or have what you want in life.

What you have just written was the old story that you have told so many times that you eventually started believing it yourself.

Now it's time to write the new story…

We will do that in Chapter 10.

Pillar V

Visualize Your Future

Chapter 9

See It Happening Now

So, what does it mean to Visualize? Visualization is simply creating a mental "picture" of what you want to accomplish, change, design, or discover. When you create your mental picture, make it as real as possible. Even if you don't believe this "thing" can happen or come true. Some people do better with connecting to the feeling instead of the mental picture. This works just as well. Use all your senses - touching, seeing, hearing, smelling, and tasting. Use whatever works best for you to evoke the feelings and emotions associated with the thing you are imagining.

Numerous studies have proven that visualization can be just as effective in improving skills vs. practicing skills. Many famous athletes use visualization to stay at the top of their game. Some people use visualization to eliminate headaches, reduce stress and anxiety, to ease stiff and tight muscles as well as help their body heal faster.

Science has proven that the mind does not distinguish between something that you've experienced and something you've only imagined. Because of this, visualization works to train the mind and body to believe you have already done the thing you visualize, perhaps many times over.

Our brain has a filter that helps us sift through and organize billions of bits of data. It's called the reticular activating system (RAS). Your RAS is a bundle of nerves at our brainstem that filters out unnecessary information, so the relevant information gets through. Your RAS is always on your side, looking to prove you right to validate your beliefs whether these beliefs are good or bad.

You'll only notice what you focus on. I'll say that one more time. You'll only notice what you focus on... Let that sink in.

And what you put your attention on becomes very real to you. If you focus on pain, worry, and anxiety, your RAS will seek to find things in alignment with these thoughts. It filters the world through the parameters you give it, and your beliefs shape those parameters.

If you think you will be in debt forever, you probably will be. If you believe you will never lose weight, you probably won't. If you are so sure you are going to get that new job or promotion, you probably will get it. If you think all marriages end in divorce, yours likely will too. The RAS helps you see what you want to see and, in doing so, influences your behaviors, thoughts, and actions.

"Though No One Can Go Back And Make A Brand New Start, Anyone Can Start From Now And Make A Brand New Ending." — Carl Bard

---

Let's do this! Think of the goal or experience you want to create. Visualize where you want to be and what you want to accomplish. Create a mental picture of how you would love that goal or experience to turn out. See yourself living the life you have always wanted. Visualize and focus on precisely what you would like to happen.

Remember, you want to focus on your purpose, not on your problems. Whatever you consistently see in your mind manifests into reality.

What does it look like? Where would you be? What would an ideal day look like to you? Who would you be with? What would you be doing?

Answer the following:

What would an ideal DAY look like to you?

_____

_____

_____

How would your ideal DAY be different than it is right now?

_____

_____

_____

What would an ideal LIFE look like to you?

_____

_____

_____

How would your ideal LIFE be different than it is right now?

_____

_____

_____

List three goals you would like to achieve in the next year.

_____

_____

_____

What is the work that needs to be done to achieve those goals in the
next year?

_____

_____

_____

How important are these goals, and why? What will happen as a result
of achieving these goals?

_____

_____

_____

Name a few obstacles that might occur while working on these goals.

_____

_____

_____

How will you overcome these obstacles? What is your plan? What will you do to ensure you never stay knocked down?

_____

_____

_____

It is a good practice to break down larger goals into multiple, smaller goals, so they are easier to manage and attain. As you achieve each smaller goal, you will build momentum towards the grand picture without overwhelming yourself and giving up.

Your goals should make you want to jump out of bed, excited to work on them every day. Do not create goals from what you think you "should" be doing or what others think you should be doing. Create goals from what calls to your heart. If not, you will never follow through when things get tough.

When your goals are truly aligned with your highest values, you will automatically think about them and will not have to be reminded to take action towards them. And when a challenge presents itself - you will still stay on course or adjust the course until the goal is attained.

Visualize each of your answers you have written above, see them in your mind daily and weekly. Visualize the moment you wake up and right before you go to sleep.

Pillar VI

Affirm Your Worth

Chapter 10

The Power of Your Words

We have covered so far how the subconscious mind records every event throughout your life. Now let's talk about the power of your words when it comes to the subconscious mind.

Your subconscious mind is a perfect goal-seeking machine. At every moment, it creates your life reality based on the picture of yourself and your life that is held in your subconscious mind.

Your mind is always at work, creating what you tell it to manifest in your life. Every statement you make to yourself or others leaves an imprint on your mind. Words that you keep repeating over time, whether true or false, will become a part of your belief system.

If you are not getting the results you want, then listen to your own words. Learn to use your language for positive results every day. You can program your mind to create changes in your reality.

"All Truths Are Easy To Understand Once They Are Discovered; The Point Is To Discover Them." — Galileo Galilei

---

Affirmations are a way to autocorrect your self-talk. When you say or write your affirmations, you are giving instructions to your subconscious mind. We have covered that the subconscious mind gives all messages equal weight. Giving it positive input consistently in the form of affirmations helps rewire or redirect those old thoughts that have kept you stuck in a rut.

I remember the first time I created an affirmation poster. I was at an event, and I was asked to create a poster full of positive words that described myself. I couldn't write one word without crying. I didn't believe one word I was writing. I had to keep looking at other people's posters to get ideas on what to say about myself. It was right then and there that I realized I had lost all self-love. I had not peeled back all the layers yet and faced them one by one. I had not fully forgiven myself for the mistakes or bad judgments I had made in the past. And, I had not fully forgiven the people and events that had hurt me in the past. I was carrying around all this extra baggage in my head without realizing it.

If you're struggling with creating affirmations - what is it that is holding you back? What thoughts are coming to mind when you start to write your affirmations? Why will you not allow yourself to believe? Go back to Chapter 8 on Forgiveness and fill out those answers. Re-read your answers daily until you feel a new shift in your thinking.

Let's give this a go! For new inspiring actions to arise in you, every day, say the same inspirational affirmations. Emphatically declare to yourself daily that you have the power to change your life.

Here are a few tools that have helped my clients as well as myself:

BE PRESENT: Affirmations must be stated in the present tense because your subconscious mind is quite literal. If you say something like, "I'm going to start a new business that makes a lot of money." The message you are sending to your mind is that you will be there someday, but not now. You want the subconscious to believe it is happening now. So instead, state your affirmations closer to things like, "I have started a new successful business that brings in unlimited income."

BE POSITIVE: State affirmations in the positive. The subconscious mind does not comprehend concepts like "not," "don't," and other negative qualifiers. If someone says to you, "Don't think about a yellow bus," what happens? You think of a yellow bus. Your mind completely ignores the word "don't." Always create a picture of what you want, not what you don't want. So, instead of saying things like "I don't waste money like I used to," replace with "I am taking charge of my finances and, I am accumulating more wealth."

BE SPECIFIC: Since your subconscious mind is an excellent engine for creating your reality, be sure you are precise and exact about the reality you say you want. Don't say, "I have a new house," when you mean to say, "I have a beautiful new house with an incredible view that has 3 bedrooms, a two-car garage, and a pool in the backyard."

FEEL IT: Use words that ignite feelings of love and inspiration. Use words you can link to sensory associations such as seeing, hearing, speaking, feeling as well as aroma, taste, and location.

PRACTICE IT: Say or write your affirmations out several times a day. Pick one place or time you can remember to do this (taking a shower, driving in the car, brushing your teeth, etc.). When you do this, take a moment to visualize what you are saying or writing. Affirmations work best when you create the reality in your mind each time you use them.

Short affirmations like these are great when you need a quick reminder to get back on track. You can say them to yourself while in your car or on the go:

I AM STRONG	I AM UNSTOPPABLE
I AM POWERFUL	I AM CREATIVE
I AM SPONTANEOUS	I AM ENERGETIC
I AM HEALTHY	I AM A GO GETTER
I AM VIBRANT	I AM YOUNG
I AM DESIRABLE	I AM LOVED

Now create your own:

I AM _____	I AM _____
I AM _____	I AM _____
I AM _____	I AM _____
I AM _____	I AM _____

Dr. John Demartini of the movie ***The Secret*** and author of many best-selling books reports that the ancients knew the power of writing. They found that when you put it in writing how you want your life to be, you reach past all fear and uncertainty into a higher realm of accomplishment. And through your written words, you dissolve all obstacles and barriers on the visible and invisible planes of life.

"Determine That The Thing Can And Shall Be Done,

And Then We Shall Find The Way." — *Abraham Lincoln*

Now that we understand affirmations write down what you want your life to be like in each of the following categories. Remember to write your affirmations in the present tense as if they are already real and happening.

A few more examples:

- "With each and every day, my health is improving, and I am getting stronger."
- "I am in a loving relationship with a partner that fully supports my wants and needs."
- "I am a successful money manager and always make smart financial decisions."
- "My relationship with my children is healthy and loving, and we have great communication."

Let's give this a go! Write at least two to three affirmations in each category.

FAMILY:

CAREER:

_____

_____

_____

SOCIAL/FRIENDS:

_____

_____

_____

HEALTH:

_____

_____

_____

SPIRITUAL:

_____

_____

_____

MENTAL OUTLOOK:

_____

_____

_____

FINANCIAL:

_____

_____

_____

Remember that old story you used to walk around repeating about yourself in Chapter 8?

Now is the time to change your destiny! Write a new story that starts from right now!

Write your new story in the present tense as if it's already happening. Take all the categories we just covered and sum them up in two or three powerful sentences that you can remember and repeat to yourself daily.

Here's your defining moment... Finish the following statement:

"I AM NOW:"

_____

_____

_____

_____

_____

_____

_____

_____

_____

_____

_____

_____

_____

_____

Now start speaking to yourself daily - being, acting, and feeling who you want to be.

At least once a day, go back and re-read the things you have written and then visualize how you are going to achieve your goals.

Dedicate at least one hour or more per day towards working on your goals. Take small action steps each day towards those goals until you have achieved them.

It's important to remember that there might be people, events, and tragedies in our lives that could challenge our positive outlook in the coming years.

We can stick our heads in the sand and pretend like nothing bad is ever going to happen in the future. Or we can create a backup plan and know we have procedures in place should unexpected emergencies come up.

So, it's a good idea to write down how you will handle unforeseen situations in your affirmations. Design a plan B for how you will manage issues with your career, your family, your health, your finances, etc.

Pillar VII

Be Grateful
For Everything

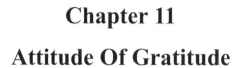

Chapter 11

Attitude Of Gratitude

If I were to take all my life lessons and experiences and sum up my life in one word, it would have to be: gratitude. I would not be the person I am today without each and every trial and tribulation. And I probably wouldn't be writing this book and helping others this way if my life had been all unicorns and rainbows! Ha!

All the highs and all the lows we experience throughout our lives are what makes every one of us unique. It's what we do with those experiences that make all the difference.

Many of us get caught up in the whirlwind and daily stresses of life. We forget to pause and take a moment to be in the present. We overlook the simplest and most important things, such as just being alive and being able to breathe, see, speak, hear, walk, and so much more.

If you want to make significant changes in your life, you must find the inner strength to be grateful. You get to make the choice. Do you want to keep retelling your old story of what you can not have, be or do? Or do you want to be the one that changes your destiny?

Whatever you are going through - the loss of a job, a divorce, a disease, an injury, a tragic event, or even being stuck in the past. When you stop to find the "lesson" in that situation, you will then see the "gift." Ask yourself, "How has this made me stronger? What have I learned from it? What will I do differently next time? And lastly, how can I help someone else going through the same thing?"

By developing an attitude of sincere gratitude, you will tap into a source of abundance like never before and you will attract more for which you can be grateful.

Think about the things you love and enjoy, not the things that cause you stress or anxiety. You will always move in the direction of your most dominant thoughts. When you take time to regularly focus on the things in your life that you are grateful for, your perspective shifts to a more positive place.

Studies have shown that having gratitude affects the brain's reward system. It promotes the release of dopamine and serotonin. Serotonin is a neurotransmitter that activates the happiness center of your brain. Dopamine is what makes you feel good and causes you to want more.

Dopamine and serotonin are chemical messengers that carry electrical signals between neurons in the brain. Imbalances with dopamine and serotonin affect your mood, memory, sleep, appetite, sex drive, and so much more.

Your brain cannot focus on positive and negative things at the same time. This is a crucial reason why practicing gratitude can help you shift your focus from being sad about the things you don't have in your life to being glad for the things you do have.

Have gratitude for where you are - good or bad. No matter where you are in life - there will always be someone who has it worse than you. Give thanks for where you are now and give thanks for the significant changes you are making.

"It's Not Happiness That Brings Us Gratitude.
It's Gratitude That Brings Us Happiness." — Unknown

JOURNALING
I have so many great mentors in my life, and all of them say the same thing - that journaling continues to be extremely instrumental in their roads to success.

Here are just a few of the many benefits of journaling:

- It helps clarify any issue in your life
- Promotes breakthroughs and insights
- Awakens the inner voice
- Acts as your own counselor
- Releases thoughts or emotions
- Enhances self-expression
- Better sleep and dreams
- Plants seeds of the future
- Deeper level of learning
- Provides Stability

And it's not just journaling that's good for you. To be more specific, I am talking about keeping a gratitude journal. A gratitude journal puts you in a different mental state. You're not keeping tabs all the things that went wrong in your day and all the people who upset you. Instead, you are recapping the things that you are grateful for and the things that bring you joy.

If you find you need to vent out something bad that happened - then find the lesson or the message in what happened that day. What did you learn from this experience? What will you do differently next time?

Keeping a gratitude journal also helps reduce stress and create feelings of peace and serenity. According to neuroscience, when we feel and express gratitude, our hypothalamus is activated. This part of our brain controls a range of different body functions, including emotional regulation. So, the more you focus on what you're thankful for, the more likely you are to adjust your reactions to daily situations.

Don't just think grateful thoughts - write it out! There is a connection between writing the gratitude statement and the subconscious mind. The goal of the exercise is to remember a good event, experience, person, or thing in your life - then imprint it in your mind, then enjoy the good emotions that come with it.

Tips for your gratitude journal: Make it a daily habit to write in your journal first thing in the morning. This helps to start your day grounded and centered. Practice appreciating the big and small things. Everything from your family, friends, and health to your dog, the weather, hot showers, and your comfy bed! Appreciate the good as well as the not so great days and what you learned from each day. It helps to pick one thing and go into super detail on why that thing, person, or event was so special. The more great things you write about, the more wonderful things you will attract into your life.

So, now you give it a try. Finish the following statement.

"I Am So Thankful And Grateful For:"

_____

_____

_____

_____

_____

_____

_____

_____

_____

_____

_____

_____

If you are having a hard time completing this drill - chances are you are still stuck in your old "story." Let's talk about that...

Most of us tell a negative story of our past and how it's held us back. We repeat this dramatic monologue many times over instead of telling the story of the future and what we want to create or what we want to become.

Remember my client Marie? She was doing the same thing until she became grateful and started focusing on her future versus her past problems.

Have gratitude for what you think is holding you back or what you think is your enemy. What if you found the "gift" in that tragedy, that event, or that person who hurt you?

What if you were equally conscious of the upsides vs. only the downsides of that person or event? Once you do, you will find it easier to have a sense of gratitude - about everything!

Continue writing your gratitude statements daily and re-read them as often as you can. It helps to get a separate notebook that is solely for your gratitude journal.

Pillar VIII

Get Grounded
In Meditation

Chapter 12

Meditation: The Missing Link

What if there was a way you could keep yourself from diving into the ditch of negativity when something unexpected happens? What if there was something you could do each day that could help you stay on track no matter what you are going through?

If I could pinpoint the one thing that has helped me overcome and get through the toughest times, I would have to say it is meditation and prayer. Prayer is what helped me have faith that better days were ahead. Meditation is what kept me sane as I was having setbacks and feeling like my life was spiraling out of control.

What's crazy is, I did not fully comprehend the benefits until I started meditating daily. Now, I am so addicted that if I skip a day - I feel like something is out of place.

To meditate is the act of using techniques intended to encourage a heightened state of awareness. In other words, meditation can calm our minds and improve our mental focus.

Meditation has been practiced in cultures all over the world for thousands of years. Nearly every religion, including Buddhism, Hinduism, Christianity, Judaism, and Islam, has a tradition of using meditation. And many people practice meditation independently of any religious or spiritual practices.

Research has shown that meditation can have both physiological and psychological effects.

Here are just a few of the many benefits of practicing meditation:

- Reduced respiration rate

- Stress reduction

- Increased self-awareness

- Improved emotional wellbeing

- Pain relief

- Better attention span

- Improved concentration

- Lower heart rate

- Better sleep

- Better stress management skills

- Improvement in memory

- Reduced feelings of depression

- Change in brain wave patterns

- Less irritable and calmer

"Meditation Brings Wisdom; Lack of Meditation Leaves Ignorance. Know Well What Leads You Forward And What Holds You Back, And Choose The Path That Leads To Wisdom." — Buddha

---

"Mindful breathing" is the most common meditation technique, and it is simple and easy to learn. When you are mindfully aware of your breath, you get into a relaxed zone that starts almost immediately.

"Mindful body scan" is the exercise of scanning your body with awareness and noticing various sensations such as body temperature, heaviness, discomfort, stiffness, and so on. Basically, you're taking inventory on what's going on in your body and where you need to send light, love, and healing.

Do you have back pain? Have trouble sleeping? Get headaches often? Got a burn or cut on your body? Got a cold sore on your lip? The mindful body scan is a very beneficial technique that helps you zero in on a specific area so you can send your team of healthy cells to the frontline to start the healing process.

I have used this technique for years to help with anxiety, stress, back pain, arthritis pain, for sleeping deeper, for anti-aging, as well as helping me to wake up with more energy.

The more you meditate, the greater your focus will become. You will soon find yourself craving your daily meditations because it helps you reduce stress and feel relaxed. You'll feel the benefits not just during the meditation - but throughout your whole day.

My favorite resource for meditations is on Youtube, where you will find the best "meditation gurus" available today. These beautiful souls invest numerous hours, creating the most unique and mind-altering meditations and provide them for free. Some meditations will have music and tones only (with no spoken words). And then other meditations will have guided recordings where they will talk you through the meditation (also with music and certain tones).

There are meditations for sleeping, pain relief, anxiety, depression, anti-aging, boosting energy, increasing abundance, and so much more. There are even unique frequencies of music where all you have to do is just listen to these specific tones, and your body and mind will start to relax and start its repairing process. For more info on different types of meditations - see the resources page in the back of this book.

As a newbie, you might discover you can unwind quickly. If so, this will allow your body and mind to become receptive to the meditation from the start. Other people may find it takes them ten to thirty minutes or more before their mind slows down enough to start meditating. But with continued practice, meditation gets easier, more comfortable, and its benefits become more profound.

Every morning I like to listen to a "gratitude meditation." It starts me off in such a great mood, boosts my energy, and makes me feel like I can conquer anything. In the evening, I listen to my favorite "healing cells meditation." It trains my subconscious mind to rally the troops of healthy cells and send them throughout my body to start the healing and repair process from a long day of work, strenuous exercise, and stress.

Your body has the intuition to heal itself. Your brain is your control center. All you need to do is guide it with the correct thoughts and vibrations. Whatever you do, don't overthink it. You can do this! Start with a simple, five minutes guided meditation, and then you can practice longer meditations as the days go by.

Pillar IX

Find A Mentor

Chapter 13

Growing Beyond Your Wildest Dreams

Some people work well with reading books and materials and doing personal transformation work on their own. They are good self-starters and self-motivators. They just need the elements, and they'll take it from there and will follow the necessary steps to make changes. If this is you, then this book might be all you need. Congrats!

Others like to have someone more involved in their life, someone they can talk to either by phone, an online video meeting, or in-person to get weekly feedback and direction. The biggest reason they need a personal connection is that they need someone who will hold them accountable.

Truth be told – it is the majority of us that need an accountability partner!

Life can be very challenging. We all have so many obligations and pressure in our lives. Month after month, week after week, things keep piling up. And the next thing you know, those dreams of starting a project, going back to school, flying home to see your parents, learning how to speak another language, learning a new skill, taking a vacation in another country, and so much more all get put on the back burner.

It seems like every time we blink our eyes another month, and another year has passed. And the feeling of disappointment grows.

We stop pursuing our dreams, we stop exercising, we stop eating healthy, we stop learning new things, and we go back to our comfort zone. We waste time with social media, binge-watching TV, playing video games, and more.

That's the reason why a life coach or mentor is so important. We often get so set in our ways that it's hard to see things from a fresh perspective. It's nearly impossible to comprehend the opportunities and the possibilities that are out there waiting for us when we're so used to being stuck in our comfort zone and our old way of thinking for so long.

"For What It's Worth: It's Never Too Late To Be Whoever You Want To Be. I Hope You Live A Life You're Proud Of, And If You Find You're Not, I Hope You Have The Strength To Start Over Again." — F. Scott Fitzgerald

---

How can a coach or mentor help you? The list is endless, but here are a few worth mentioning:

- Taking business to the next level
- Following through with goals
- Getting rid of limiting beliefs
- Unable to define a plan
- Wasting time on unimportant things
- Don't have family or spouse support
- Improving health and longevity
- Don't know where to begin
- Need to reduce anxiety and stress
- Finances/career are in disarray
- Lacking passion or motivation
- Wanting to leave a legacy

I hired my first mentor when I finally accepted that it was time to make massive changes in my life. I still have mentors today and will never break the momentum I have created. I've seen too many benefits and have experienced too many breakthroughs to stop the progress!

There are a few things to keep in mind when looking for a mentor. Find someone you resonate with. Maybe it's someone you work with. Perhaps it's an author or other expert you have wanted to meet. Maybe it's a coach you saw on Youtube or Facebook. There are many great mentors, coaches, leaders, online experts, etc. Some give free advice on their Youtube channels or in their Facebook groups. And if you need more in-depth guidance, many of these experts offer private coaching and group coaching.

You might get lucky and find more than one mentor that really inspires you. Just make sure you enjoy their voice, their presence as well as their mission. If you are not in alignment with their thoughts and actions, you will soon find yourself not coming back to finish the courses you bought. And possibly wasting the money you invested.

Remember to take one step at a time. Don't overwhelm yourself by getting consumed on the big picture. Take small steps to accomplish your end goals. There will be bumps in the road, and creating your new life might not happen overnight.

Give yourself some grace and patience. All it takes is putting one foot in front of the other and just taking one more step, get up one more time, do one more rep and give it one more shot, etc.

But whatever you do - don't quit! Every time you stop, you lose momentum. And time is the most precious commodity that you will never be able to replenish.

Start surrounding yourself with like-minded people who want more out of life. Cut out all toxic people and influences. Refuse to let old thought patterns creep back in, refuse to let the old toxic conversations to replay in your mind...

That's when your life will come back around... Doors will start opening; new opportunities will start coming your way.

And that's all I want for you - is an Encore... Your incredible, fantastic, out of this world Epic Encore that makes you want to get out of bed excited for all the wonderful moments coming your way!

So, let's help you get your health, wealth, and mental focus back or anything else you want to work on. It's time to create YOUR EPIC ENCORE!

Start filling out the answers in this book today! I would love to hear your success stories!

To get more info on mentoring or to share your story, send an email to Cheryl@YourEpicEncore.com

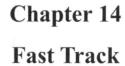

Chapter 14

Fast Track

Reinventing yourself or creating Your Epic Encore might not happen overnight, but there are a few techniques you can implement to speed up the process. Remember, it's the little steps you take each day that will create a massive compound effect.

Here are a few rules or guidelines to help you stay on track daily:

Be Impeccable With Your Word. Say what you mean and mean what you say. Once you start holding yourself to a higher standard, you will stop making promises you can't keep, and you will become a more reliable person. You will also stop saying things you don't mean, and you will attract other honorable people and friends with like-minded values who will support you, not bring you down.

Finish What You Start - How many times have you started to make a change, and then things got rough, and you stopped? Do not allow yourself to quit. Challenges will come, and obstacles will present themselves. It takes dedication and patience. Make a promise to yourself that you will not throw in the towel when things get hard. Always keep this mind: time is your most precious commodity - don't waste it; you must treasure it!

Do Everything Differently - Breaking out your comfort zone forces you to have new experiences, meet new people, and learn something new. Take a Sunday drive to somewhere you've never been. Listen to a different type of music, get your groceries at a new grocery store and shop for clothes at a different store. Get a new hair cut or color or get your hair done at a different salon or barbershop. Rearrange the furniture in your house, add a plant, replace old couch pillows, or add new lighting to a room. Trade-in that old car that reminds you of your past relationship, etc.

Keep The Engine Revved Up - Never stop learning. Read books on personal development or business or whatever interests you. Learn a new language or take up a new hobby. Attend a workshop, webinar, or local college class. Not only will you learn new skills, but you will also meet new people. Just keep learning new things. Every time you do, you'll help increase the number of synapses between your neurons in the brain, allowing them to send and receive information faster. This helps with brain neuroplasticity and keeps the brain sharp!

Get Rid Of The Junk - Clean your house, your kitchen, your family room, your bedroom, your closet, your drawers, your garage, and so on. Donate clothes, shoes, purses, ties, and belts you haven't used in years to Salvation Army or call a junk removal service for bigger items. Cleaning up your environment also clears your mind at the same time. A study at Princeton University Neuroscience Institute proved all that "stuff" is a distraction from what we would otherwise concentrate on. Therefore, our productivity decreases while our anxiety increases. So, clean it up!

Fix Things That Are Broken. You cannot focus 100% on what you want to do if you are constantly distracted, thinking about the things in your house, garage, or office that need to be repaired. Call the handyman - get the broken window replaced, repair the garage door that won't shut, fix the home camera that stopped working, and the faucet that keeps leaking, etc.

Make New Friends. Find people that have the same common interests. Social media has made it very easy to meet people from all over the world. Find events that pique your curiosity, challenge you and help you grow. Do you collect butterflies, weird stamps, bottle caps, or have a goal to see every art museum in the US? I guarantee you there is someone else who wants to do that too! There are specialized groups inside Facebook, Pinterest, Instagram, and more where you can engage with like-minded people and get invited to unique events, online workshops and groups.

- **Make Friends With Younger People** - or Younger Minded People. Studies have shown that you are the company you keep. Most younger individuals haven't fallen into the trap of "Oh, I'm too old to do that." Younger minded friends will invite you to go skiing, skydiving, white water rafting, frisbee golf, and more. Your older minded friends most likely will be complaining about illness, stiff joints, and things that aren't working well in their bodies anymore. Don't fall into that trap. If you think young, healthy thoughts, you will create younger, healthy cells.

- **Do Something That Excites You** - or even scares you a little bit. Go skydiving, bungee jumping, go to a mermaid/merman school, go roller skating, snow skiing, paddle boarding, try yoga or aerial yoga, take a painting class or a pottery class. Sign up for private lessons or a weekend course on something you would normally never try! And if you are visiting or live in the Los Angeles area - try an aerial class with me! (See my info in the back of the book).

- **Manage Your Moo-la** - Making a new start might involve making new purchases. If you want to change careers, you might need to invest in workshops, college, or online courses. Create a self-transformation budget and stick to it.

- **Manage Your Stress & Sleep -** High-stress levels and lack of sleep can cause serious health issues, from weakened immunity to heart problems. Get at least 7-8 hours of sleep. Take measures to monitor and control your stress. If you can't get a handle on your sleep cycles or stress levels - go back to the section on meditation. Once you start connecting and getting the feel of meditation, you will be surprised how something so easy and so simple can change your life. Remember, your mind is one powerful engine. But it's up to you to re-train it to bring about thoughts you enjoy.

- **Exercise and Eat Healthier -** If you are not taking care of your vessel, it will not take care of you. Exercise strengthens your immune system, your cardio health, your muscle strength, and it helps releases endorphins that make you happy. Many of our health problems can be traced back to not eating healthy, not exercising, and over use of alcohol and cigarettes. Make it a goal to stop eating processed packaged foods, fast foods, fried foods, sweets, etc. Try to incorporate more whole foods, more vegetables, more fruits, and less red meat. Choose organic foods and store food in glass containers vs. plastic. Drink filtered water. If you would like to know which water filter I use - see the back of the book.

Be Kind & Nourish Your Soul - Volunteering is not just good for others; it's good for your soul. It gives you a sense of purpose, fulfills your heart, and makes you happy. Look for volunteer opportunities in your local community that pique your interest. You'll learn new skills while creating a new social outlet. Plus, it helps us feel more positive about the world and our contribution to it too. See resources for more volunteer info.

Create Your Vision Board - Vision boards give you permission to dream and to have whatever you want. These boards help your mind to see "it" before it happens. When you give your mind something to focus on daily, it increases the probability of it manifesting. The vision directs us, makes us feel excited, and keeps us motivated because we "see" that it's entirely possible. We have visual proof. So, start collecting magazine clippings and print photos from the internet of the things you desire. Put these images on a poster board or corkboard. Hang your board in a spot where you will see daily.

Twenty-One Days - Studies have shown it takes at least 21 days of daily practice to create a new habit. If you find yourself forgetting or not repeating this habit for one month, then it probably wasn't high on your values list. Go back and find a new habit or improvement you want to implement that has true value to you. Just stick to it! If you catch yourself sliding, re-read this book and your answers as often as needed. Don't let anything slow you down or get in your way. You deserve **Your Epic Encore!** Go make it happen!

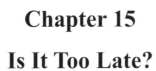

Chapter 15

Is It Too Late?

There used to be moments when I would think it's too late to start over. It's too late to start a new career; it's too late to find an ideal mate, it's too late to whatever - just fill in the blank! 'lol'

That's why I have constantly surrounded myself with clippings, articles of amazing "goal-getters" who are older than me. I get so inspired by those who have accomplished amazing feats during what is considered "late in life."

So, how about you?

What is going to keep you inspired?

What is going to keep you believing that it's never too late?

What is going to be your greatest, most incredible achievement ever?

What is going to be your legacy? What will you create and leave behind?

"It's Never Too Late To Be What You Might Have Been."

— George Eliot

Think it's too late to have an Epic Encore? Think Again! Here are just a few of the many different role models throughout history who did not get started or did not reach the height of their careers until after their 40's, 50's, 60's and later!

Julia Child - Age 50

Many of us know Julia Child as one of the first celebrity chefs with her cookbooks and a TV show. What most people don't know is that she was pretty bad at cooking in her 30's. Right after graduation, Julia worked as a copywriter, and during World War II, she was a spy. In 1948 she attended the Cordon Bleu cooking school. Julia wrote her first cookbook at 50 years old and launched her career as a chef in 1961. She wrote 19 cookbooks, created thirteen TV shows, and accumulated a net worth of 38 million

Susan Boyle - Age 47

For many years, the Scottish singer Susan Boyle was unknown for her amazing voice. However, things completely changed in April of 2009 when she appeared on Britain's Got Talent. Her debut studio album, *I Dreamed a Dream*, was released in November 2009 and became the UK's best-selling debut album of all time. Topping the *Billboard* 200 for six weeks and was the second best-selling album of 2009 in the US. At age 47, Susan thought she was too old to be on Britain's Got Talent. But her coach persuaded her to audition, and now she is one of the most famous contestants and has a net worth of 40 million.

Colonel Sanders - Age 65

Harland Sanders didn't become the mogul we know and love until he was 65. He held many jobs over the years. He was a fireman, steam engine stoker, insurance salesman, he even practiced law and was fired a few times. In 1952 he perfected his spice blend and quick-cooking technique for making fried chicken. Then he went on the road and started selling franchises named Kentucky Fried Chicken. In 1964 there were over 900 locations, and he sold KFC for $2 million.

Anna Mary Robertson Moses - Age 78

Most of us know Anna Mary Robertson, one of the biggest names in American folk art as Grandma Moses. She had been a fan of embroidery for many years. But once it became too painful for her to hold a needle, she transitioned to painting. She was 78 when she created her first painting. Her works have been shown in the United States and abroad and have been printed on various merchandise as well as on greeting cards. Many museums display Grandma Moses' paintings still today. The most extensive collection of paintings by Grandma Moses is at the Bennington Museum in Bennington, Vermont.

Laura Ingalls Wilder - Age 65
Wilder's *Little House on the Prairie* is one of the world's most beloved children's books. Wilder didn't publish her first novel until she was 65 years old, and she still managed to write 12 books in her series, although some were published after her passing. Wilder began writing her autobiography, titled *Pioneer Girl* in her 60's. Publishers rejected it. So, she rewrote most of her stories for children. The result was the *Little House* series of books, which have been continuously in print and have been translated into 40 other languages.

Vera Wang - Age 40
Before she was one of the most famous bridal and fashion designers, Vera Wang was a competitive figure skater and a journalist. Vera graduated from Sarah Lawrence College with an Art History degree. She was then hired to be an editor at Vogue, where she became the senior fashion editor. Vera stayed at Vogue for 17 years, leaving in 1987 to join Ralph Lauren, for whom she worked for two years. At age forty, Vera resigned and became an independent designer for bridal wear carrying her name. As of 2020, Vera wang has an estimated net worth of 650 million.

Samuel L Jackson - Age 45
Samuel L. Jackson is known as one of the highest-grossing actors of all time who has starred in over 100 movies. Jackson attended Morehouse College and majored in marine biology. He then transitioned to architecture and later settled on drama after taking a public speaking class in his 20's. Although he had acted in many movies, it wasn't until Jackson's thirtieth film (Pulp Fiction) that he was internationally recognized and received praise from critics - this was at the age of 45. In 2011 he was named the highest-paid actor with more than $7.1 billion total in US box office gross.

John Bannister Goodenough - Age 97
John is an American materials scientist and a solid-state physicist. He is a mechanical engineering professor in Texas and has been credited with the

development of the lithium-ion battery. John also developed the Goodenough–Kanamori rules in determining the sign of the magnetic superexchange in materials and seminal developments in computer random access memory. In 2019, he became the oldest Nobel laureate in history and was awarded the Nobel Prize in Chemistry, at 97 years old.

Pretty cool stories, right? As you have just heard, it's never too late to start something new.

It's never too late to switch gears or to start over, or to go in another direction.

Life is a constant journey and it's up to us to find the gifts or the lessons in every situation. It's how we use those lessons to help others that makes all the difference.

To wrap up this book, I have a fun visualization drill for you.

Let's imagine that it's 10, 20, or even 30 or more years from now...

Visualize your future...

What will you be known for?

Which obstacles will you overcome?

What's Your "Thing?"

What do you want to discover, create or explore?

What is the legacy you are going to build and leave behind for others?

On the next page will be a few visualization sentences.

These will sound similar to the stories you have just read.

Fill in the blanks with your answers. Here we go:

Your Name_____ did not _____

his/her first _____ until he/she was age

_____ . He/she held many _____ in the

beginning. He/she was once a _____

_____

but one day decided to follow his/her passions and _____

_____

_____

that we now know today as _____

_____ .

He/she also went on to _____

and _____

_____ and fulfilled his/her lifelong dreams!

Great Job! You made it to the end! Be sure to revisit your answers,
and the skills and techniques in this book as often as possible.

Repetition is the key to making life long changes. Keep repeating until
this becomes a natural part of your daily lifestyle.

You can do this! Keep me posted! I can't wait to hear how you created
YOUR EPIC ENCORE!

Thank You For Reading Your Epic Encore!
I Hope This Book Has Helped You In Some
Way Like It Has Helped Me.

Never Stop Dreaming, Never Stop Believing!
It's Never Too Late To Have YOUR EPIC ENCORE!

With Deepest Love & Respect,

Cheryl Broughton
Author, Aerialist & Coach
53 years YOUNG!

**To Those Who Have Read My Book
I'd Like To Reward You With Two Free Bonuses!**

**BONUS #1:
You are getting free access to my Facebook group!
You'll get to take advantage of exclusive trainings,
private interviews, beta course launches and so much more!**

**Go To:
facebook.com/Groups/YourEpicEncore/**

**BONUS #2:
You are getting access to a special bonus course
I made just for those who have read the book!**

**Go To:
YourEpicEncore.com/Bonus**

**I can t wait to hear your success stories!
You can share them inside the Facebook group -
or send an email to cheryl@YourEpicEncore.com**

**While on social media, feel free to take pictures of yourself
with my book and make sure to tag: @YourEpicEncore**

**It's Never Too Late
To Have
YOUR
EPIC
ENCORE!**

Resources

For more information on Cheryl's programs, books, events and more: Go to CherylBroughton.com or YourEpicEncore.com or go to Facebook and Instagram and search: @YourEpicEncore and @CherylBroughton or Facebook.com/groups/YourEpicEncore/

Recommended Books & Programs:
- *The Four Agreements* - By Don Miguel Ruiz
- *The Values Factor* - By Dr. John Demartini
- *Loving Yourself - It's An Inside Job* - By Kareen Borzone
- *Volunteering Skills That Last You A Lifetime. Become The Entrepreneur That Changes Lives* - By Jay Williamson
- *How to Transform Wounds To Wisdom and Create A New Life* - By Subira Folami
- Staying35ish.com - Aging Is Optional - By Candice Morgan
- Adventure2Vitality.com - by Alexa Freeburg
- SingleLadiesRock.com - On A Mission of TRUTH - To Discover, Explain & Empower By Wendy Lehn
- EdyMade.com - by Edy Pickens. Edy is changing the world by creating and teaching art as a means to heal depression. She inspires others to make their art and use it for healing purposes.

Meditations:
- Here are some of my favorite guided meditation gurus: Go to youtube.com and type in Michael Sealey, Jason Stephenson, Power Thoughts Meditation Club, Kenneth Soares, Ziva Meditation with Emily Fletcher or Mindful Meditation with Sarah Ramon.
- Here are some of my favorite frequency meditations: Go to youtube.com and type in Meditative Mind, Nu Meditation Music, Body Mind Zone or Good Vibes - Binaural Beats. Or just type in 432Hz. You will find many different types of meditation music and tones with higher or lower Hz. (Hz stands for Hertz which are cycles of sound per second).

Water Filters & Vitamins:
- Want to know which water filters I use to keep my body healthy from the inside out? Or which vitamins I use for joint pain and inflammation? Go to YourEpicEncore.com or CherylBroughton.com.

Aerial Circus Lessons & Equipment:
- Want to take a private aerial circus lesson with me? Go to CircusLessons.com. You can also go to Facebook or Instagram and search @CherylTheFlyGirl
- Want to get your own Aerial rig for your house or studio? Need hardware and apparatuses too? Contact my friend Summer Davies at VerticalArtDance.com. Mention my name and this book and get a free upgrade on your order.

Celebrity Mentions/Fact Checking:
- Wikipedia.com & Biography.com

Domestic Violence Resources:

The National Domestic Violence Hotline
1-800-799-7233 (SAFE)   www.ndvh.org

National Dating Abuse Helpline
1-866-331-9474.   www.loveisrespect.org

National Suicide Prevention Lifeline
1-800-273-8255 (TALK)   www.suicidepreventionlifeline.org

National Resource Center on Domestic Violence
1-800-537-2238   www.nrcdv.org and www.vawnet.org

Futures Without Violence: The National Health Resource Center on Domestic Violence
1-888-792-2873.   www.futureswithoutviolence.org

National Center on Domestic Violence, Trauma & Mental Health
1-312-726-7020 ext. 2011.   www.nationalcenterdvtraumamh.org

Families For Depression Awareness
1-781-890-0220.   www.familyaware.org

Anxiety And Depression Association of America
1-240-485-1001.   www.adaa.org

About The Author

Cheryl Broughton has been an inspiration to thousands as an author, Fitness TV show producer and host, mind & body boot camp founder, transformation coach, aerial instructor, and professional speaker. Cheryl is the Founder of Your Epic Encore coaching and Cheryl The Fly Girl aerial training.

Cheryl has produced and hosted Fitness TV shows, infomercials, exercise DVD's and children's fitness programs. In 2001 she launched The Fitness Edge Boot Camp - a workout program that featured fitness, nutrition, and a life coaching program.

Cheryl was voted best personal trainer for seven years by The Signal Newspaper. She was also voted" Ultimate Boot Camp" by Elite Magazine and "Best Health Club" by the Signal News. She has been a published columnist for over fifteen years writing articles that focus on health, wellness, and mental focus.

In 2009 Cheryl co-founded a natural wellness company whose products are sold in health food stores across the US and are made in the USA with GMP Compliant Manufacturing.

Also in 2009, Cheryl was diagnosed with advanced arthritis and was told she needed both knees replaced. After going into a depression for some time over this - she pulled herself back up and decided to make a list of all the physical activities that one with arthritis should not be able to do, and she was determined to do them all!

Learning aerial arts was one of the things on that list. Although it was a bit challenging, it was easy on her joints, and it made her stronger and more flexible. She can now do more in her 50's than she could in her 20's!

She also studied and implemented anti-inflammatory diets, said "no" to surgery, and started taking joint supplements that helped with the pain and stiffness. She now trains, teaches, and performs in Tissu, Hoop, Hammock, and Trapeze.

When she is not coaching clients, conducting workshops or speaking, she loves to perform with VerticalArtDance.com and can be seen in remote aerial performances between mountain peaks, off the side of cliffs and over lakes - sometimes as high as 100 feet in the air!

Cheryl's message to you is this: If she can do it, so can you! It's never too late to pursue your dreams or to create *Your Epic Encore!*

WHERE'S YOUR EPIC ENCORE?

I can't wait to hear your success stories!
Send your story to Cheryl@YourEpicEncore.com and you'll
get a special training course I made just for the action takers!

Join My Free Facebook Group!

Surround yourself with other like-minded people who are living life to the fullest and not letting their age dictate what they can and can not do!

facebook.com/groups/YourEpicEncore/

Made in the USA
Coppell, TX
30 May 2021